How to Find Your Soulmate, Self-Love, and Happiness

*Love is the Key to
the Law of Attraction*

Shelley K. Martin

How to Find Your Soulmate, Self-Love, and Happiness
Love is the Key to the Law of Attraction

Categories: Motivational and Transformational Self-Help / Religion & Spirituality / Self-Esteem / Love & Relationships / Mate Seeking

FIRST EDITION
ISBN 978-0-9907531-6-2

Published in the United States by Light Post Press.

P.O. Box 2185
Denison, TX 75021

All scriptures are quoted from the King James Version of the *Holy Bible* unless otherwise noted.

Definitions and etymology referenced from John Ayto's *Dictionary of Word Origins* (1990) and *Webster's Collegiate Dictionary*.

Cover art licensed by iStock, a Getty Images company.

http://www.howtofindyoursoulmate.net

Dedication

For my daughters Lindsay and Vala, and all the sons and daughters of posterity. For my soulmate, Alan J. Martin Jr., thank you for truly loving me; without you these words would not be possible. Recognition must be given to Pamela Eakins Ph.D., a great teacher; may you be forever blessed for your relentless service to Love.

Contents

Preface

Empty yourself of your inner critic. Suspend the voice that assesses how this information fits into your beliefs. Just be present and don't think about how to defend your own deeply rooted position as you read. Keep an open mind until you've finished and you may discover something wonderful.

True love is not a strong emotional, chemical, or physical attraction. It does not need. It does not expect. True love has no agenda. It does not pretend. It will not betray you. True love will never leave you.

I knew I'd found my soulmate when I saw myself staring back through his eyes. It was as if he had become me and I was making love to myself in his body. In that mirror of perfect reflection I knew we were two halves of the same whole.

If you are searching for your soulmate, someone who adores you on the inside, sees you clearly and accepts you without condition, you've attracted the right book.

You were drawn to the truth within these pages by the <u>Universal</u> *Law of Attraction* because you are suffering, burning, questioning why the void within you feels so deep and longs to be filled.

That's what this book is about, how to stop the wanton pain of aimless wandering and realize the love and happiness that now eludes you.

You will learn what the *Law of Attraction* is, how it <u>really</u> works, and how to recognize and apply it to discovering self-love, finding your soulmate, and creating real and lasting peace, prosperity, and happiness. You will learn how to heal yourself, and in so doing you will be helping to heal the world.

I did not go to college and don't have any credentials. I chose not to pursue man's understanding in the world's institutions. I asked the Creator for wisdom, to be taught by the Great Spirit, and promised to seek truth with all of my heart and never stop.

What else is there to ask for but wisdom, if you believe God's word, which says "For wisdom is better than rubies; and all the things that may be desired are not to be compared to it" (Proverbs 8:11) and "Wisdom is the principal thing; therefore get wisdom: and with all thy getting get understanding" (Proverbs 4:7).

We can't get wisdom from school; it can only be found within. "Behold, thou desirest truth in the inward parts: and in the hidden part thou shalt make me to know wisdom" (Psalms 51:6).

It is my testimony that through what I reveal in this book, I have realized all these things in my life: self-love, a soulmate, financial security, happiness, and a peace that passes understanding. It is my mission to share the methods by which I attained such prosperity, in order to help relieve needless suffering.

I speak with authority on this subject, because I've manifested these things in my life on purpose through a process. I discovered true love in my heart, self-love and self-worth, found my soulmate, am beyond happy because I know the secret to real and lasting security, and have a dream job that allows me 100% freedom while earning top tier income.

My life experience makes me more of an authority than a scientist or therapist with no firsthand knowledge. It is said when the student is ready the teacher will come, and when the teacher is ready the student will come; and so it is.

To borrow from Pamela Eakins' *Tarot of The Spirit*, "To heal thy world, thou must heal thyself. To heal thyself, thou must know the source of thy illness. To know the source of thy illness, thou must know the Inner Self. To know the Inner Self, thou must take the Path of Spirit." I hope this helps you find your way.

When Will I Find My Soulmate?

There was a time when I wondered if every guy I was attracted to was my soulmate. I was searching for Mr. Right, and at age twenty-seven I was determined to find him. It was 1994, the year I lost my mother to ovarian cancer on her forty-seventh birthday. That's when I realized life was too short to live without passion or purpose, and I mustered the courage to admit to my then husband I was not in love with him.

He popped the question on my twenty-first birthday, family and friends looking on. We'd only been dating a couple months. I stood there stalling with gasps of surprise watching him holding the ring. My heart was urging me to say "let's wait" but I couldn't force the words past my lips. Then my dad broke the silence and asked, "Well aren't you going to answer the boy," so I said yes.

However, I was still rebounding hard, carrying a torch for my ex-boyfriend from high school. Ours was a fiery, codependent relationship based on sex and control. It began when I was sixteen and raged on and off for five years. We'd been living together and after we split he moved away and I moved back in with my parents. This time my father forbid me to see him again and the punishment for disobedience was family exile.

He was your typical bad boy, devilishly handsome and irresistibly charming until drunk. That's when he would become violent. We had some knock down drag outs. Of course he was always sorry later and would cry and say how much he loved me. Our chemistry was intoxicating and I wrongly mistook his possessiveness for love.

Obviously, it was an unhealthy relationship, so I begged God for the strength to stay away from him and to please send me my true love.

My husband was the complete opposite of my ex-boyfriend. He fit every parent's description of the perfect man for their daughter. He was loyal, a good father and stable provider. Our union lasted seven years and from it came my first born, a gift from God and my pride and joy.

Even though we split it was not a mistake; nothing really ever is. There are only opportunities for growth, but this took me a while to learn.

After I announced I wanted a divorce, I tracked down my ex-boyfriend to test the waters. He said he had also not stopped thinking about me. Convinced we were soulmates, in no time we were back together but our rekindling lasted only a year.

Nothing had really changed except that I was now a mother with a responsibility to set a good example. When I left him for good I was sick inside, punishing myself for repeated mistakes and wrecked progress.

By the time I turned thirty I had burned through five more "maybe this is the one" relationships, and that was just the beginning of my journey to find my soulmate, self-love and happiness.

In short it took more than twenty tries and a lot of heartache to find Mr. Right, so needless to say, I'm an expert on the wrong way to win a man.

Acting the sex-crazed mind blowing teaser who aims to please, with curves and a smart head for business, just isn't the magic formula. Take it from me, every time I wore that mask I lost. And I know you know that mask, every woman does at least. I call it *Seductress Syndrome*. We are taught it is how a woman should be by the media: sex sells.

I played a convincing *I can bring home the bacon, fry it up in a pan, and never ever let you forget you're a man* kind of girl. When I walked into a room both men and women turned their heads. This filled me with pride which I now know was extreme vanity.

In addition to being externally beautiful, I was a high paid executive and drove a convertible BMW. This is what I thought men wanted, a sexy, successful, strong, independent woman.

It's what society told me I should be. Even my own mother jokingly said, "Learn how to give a good blow job and you can get a man to take care of you."

But when it came to relationships I was always left wondering what was wrong with me? What was my problem? What was his? Why didn't even one of the men I so desperately yearned for turn out to be my happily-ever-after?

I was always physically desired and used, but never loved. Sound familiar?

I purchased a deck of tarot cards in 1996, desperate to uncover how a guy I was seeing at the time really felt about me. I was hoping to get inside his head, little aware I was going to be delving deep inside my own.

I eventually discovered who I really am, what my purpose is, and drew my soulmate into my life. We are married, share a deeply intimate, otherworldly connection, and made a beautiful daughter together, our love child.

I found the love, acceptance, and deep respect I craved, only after learning to give these things to myself. Once I recognized loss as an opportunity for growth and vowed never again to abandon my own heart, or to settle for less than what I deserved, everything changed.

After learning much about myself and others, I became a tarot card reader and consulted with thousands of people from across the globe through my website.

I can confidently say that love is the #1 topic for both women and men alike, yes even men. The #1 question asked was "When will I find my soulmate?" My answer was always the same, "When you find and love yourself." The next question was naturally, "How do I find myself?" or "How do I love myself?"

The purpose of this book, and my life, is to help answer these questions by aiding you along on the path of self-discovery. The search for who you are has already begun, that's why you have been drawn to this information.

I know why you're here;
An awakening is coming.
Are you ready?
If you play with fire
It will burn you to your core,
Reveal who you really are.
Everything not real will fall away
Leaving you alone with yourself.

To be born anew
You must be willing to die,
To rise from the depths of your own ashes.
Not many have the valor to walk
Through the valley of their own shadows.
You are not who you think you are
And this frightens you.
Because deep inside your soul
You know something is missing.
You know I'm right.
That something is why you came,
But it's not what you think.
It's a mystery.
Ask God to know
And the Creator will show you
Who you really are
And what you really need.

The road to self-awareness ultimately leads to an inner marriage with Divine Love; an harmonic convergence transpires within.

There is no more urgent a need than for us as individuals and collectively to awaken to the truth of who we really are and the power of love. Love is the only thing that is real and worth pursuing.

You are the ONE you are looking for, you just don't know it yet. You can harness the *Law of Attraction* to discover yourself, attract your soulmate, and find lasting happiness and prosperity, once you know how it <u>really</u> works. Proceed to find out.

How the Law of Attraction Works

You can discover yourself, find your soulmate, happiness, prosperity, and achieve your dreams, once you know what the *Law of Attraction* is and how it really works.

Quantum Physics defines the *Law of Attraction* as being the 'mutual' or 'shared in common' action by which bodies or particles tend to draw together or cohere in a mass that resists separation. In other words, it states that *like action attracts like action.*

An action is something done, an act performed, usually to accomplish a goal, some synonyms being work, movement, activity, operation, exertion, effort. Thought is an act performed ceaselessly, the action we undertake most.

Here are some statements to help clarify how the *Law of Attraction* works:

- Like action attracts like action.
- Like operation attracts like operation.
- Like frequency attracts like frequency.
- Like energy attracts like energy.
- Like being attracts like being.
- Like thought attracts like thought.
- Like belief attracts like belief.
- Like intention attracts like intention.
- Like doing attracts like doing.
- Like giving attracts like giving.

People fail in their attempts to harness the *Law of Attraction* to achieve their desires because they don't <u>really</u> understand the *like action attracts like action* part. There are many out there who will tell you that the *Law of Attraction* works by giving you what you think about most, or believe you will receive. It is said that "energy follows thought" and thought is an action, so...

1. If you focus your thoughts on what you want, create its image in your mind,

2. Can mentally see and feel yourself with it or as it,

3. And will do this faithfully with belief until it has manifested,

4. You will attract or become that which you desire.

This is true in part, but when it comes to creating with thought, the *like action attracting like action* is what gets overlooked and thus causes the failure to achieve results. Let me better explain. I can imagine anything I want using thought, and can focus on it all I want, and can truly believe it will be mine, but I still cannot create it in my life unless I am genuinely *like it in action.*

Everything we do is action, every thought, feeling, word, and deed: Anything that spends mental or physical energy. The sum total of all this doingness equates to output, what we produce or give to the world. What we output determines our energy vibration or likeness frequency, which in turn drives what we attract. We get what we give, which is what we do. *Like action attracts like action.*

Everything vibrates, the *Law of Vibration.* We each have our own frequency, vibration, or tune which is determined by the sum total of all our actions. Our past actions equal our present reality, and our present actions equal our future reality. We put out and we get back in equal measure.

You must genuinely be like that which you wish to have or be, you must be in harmony with its frequency, or in tune with its vibration or song. You must freely give that which you want to receive. *You attract what you are like, what you do, what you give, not what you want.* The law cannot be fooled! "Be not deceived; God is not mocked: for whatsoever a man soweth, that shall he also reap" (Galatians 6:7).

Beliefs drive actions; we do based on what we believe. Belief shapes reality by driving individual and collective perception and action. This is why Christ told those who came to him for healing that it was in fact "their faith" or "their belief" that had made them whole. All our actions are fruit bearing seeds that grow and multiply after their own kind, each stemming from belief about what is true and false.

I don't just think the Natural and Universal Laws are real, I <u>know</u> they are, through careful observation and experimentation in my own life. "Do you know the ordinances (laws) of the heavens?" (Job 38:33). Do not dismiss the laws of energy God set in place, learn about them to increase your understanding.

The *Law of Attraction*, also known as *Karma*, explains how and why God's justice is unwaveringly perfect. Think about it. If we always only ever receive that which we give, what could be more just?

I can think of no greater gift from our Creator than to be governed by such a fair and loving law. Our protection or destruction, our reward or punishment, is in our own hands and is based solely on what we choose to give to others of our own free will.

This is why the *Golden Rule* is so important, why Christ said "So in everything, do to others what you would have them do to you, for this sums up the Law (all the Natural and Universal Laws) and the Prophets (all the true teachings)" (Matthew 7:12).

He also says, "For in the same way you judge others, you will be judged, and with the measure you use, it will be measured to you" (Matthew 7:2). He didn't say it might be, he said it <u>will</u> be.

What you do <u>will</u> be done to you. What you give <u>will</u> return to you. This is the most urgent teaching of all true prophets, and the most important thing you need to learn and apply to everything in your life.

You may say this is not true, that many things in life seem random and unfair. For example, someone being murdered for no apparent reason when they have not murdered someone else.

The LORD said, "He that leadeth into captivity shall go into captivity: <u>he that killeth</u> with the sword <u>must be killed</u> with the sword. Here is the patience and the faith of the saints" (Revelation 13:10).

My answer to this conundrum is reincarnation. You may not believe in reincarnation, and say it's not Biblical or

Christian. However, it is the only thing that can explain many things Jesus said including the quote above.

Since this is not a book about reincarnation, I will point you to another which is, *Why Jesus Taught Reincarnation* by Herbert Bruce Puryear, Ph.D. (New Paradigm Press 1992).

The *Law of Attraction* is always at work, and influences our soul's lessons through successive lifetimes. The sooner you become aware of its governing activity the better.

The *Law of Attraction* can also be called the *Law of Giving* or the *Law of Love*. Love not only gives back to you that which you choose of your own free will to give to others, it gives you exactly what you need in every moment to move in the direction of wholeness.

You have to have the *eyes to see* (eyes of spirit) and *ears to hear* (ears of spirit) in order to recognize the healing opportunities forever being presented by the *Law of Attraction*, which is the Law of Love, true Blind Justice.

You must be willing to adjust what you are outputting if you want to change your vibration or likeness frequency and therefore what you are attracting (or inputting). Never forget, *everything vibrates*, vibration is action, and *like action attracts like action*.

Your judgments of others are mirror images in which to see your own reflection, your own likeness frequency. This is so that you can learn to adjust your actions, fine tune your vibration, and bring it into harmony with the song of love. Love is the only thing that will fill the empty void inside you. The goal is to harmonically converge with love by becoming love.

You are what you say others are. What you see in them is what you need to recognize about yourself in their mirror reflection. That which you attract, be it a thought, person, event, or circumstance, is a mirror. In that mirror you can see your soul staring back if you have the courage to open your spirit eyes and spirit ears.

Each reflection, experienced as a feeling or criticism, is an opportunity to discover who you really are on a soul level, why you are here, and what life lessons you need to master to move to the next stage on the path that ultimately leads to a marriage with Divine Love.

If what you feel to be true about anyone or anything is not in alignment with love, then those feelings are pinpointing exactly where you need to make adjustments to your own understanding.

Your beliefs about yourself and others reflect back to you whether your perception of reality is true or false, and love is the measuring rod. Love is the only truth. Everything not based in love is a lie, cannot last, and needs to be purged from each of our personalities and souls.

What is Love?

"God is love; and he that dwelleth in love dwelleth in God, and God in him" (1 John 4:16).

"Love is patient, love is kind. It does not envy, it does not boast, it is not proud. It does not dishonor others, it is not self-seeking, it is not easily angered, it keeps no record of wrongs. Love does not delight in evil but rejoices with the truth. It always protects, always trusts, always hopes, always perseveres. Love never fails" (1 Corinthians 13:4-8 NIV).

Christ said, "Love the Lord your God (who is love) with all your heart and with all your soul and with all your mind. This is the first and greatest commandment. And the second is like it (the same as it): Love your neighbor as yourself. All the Law and the Prophets hang on these two commandments" (Matthew 22:37-40).

Put love first. Serve love in everything that comes from your heart, soul, and mind. Make love your master and your guide, the only truth you live your life by. To love others, all you have to do is treat them the way you want to be treated. It's really that simple.

If you do this you will be loving God to your utmost ability and loving others as you love yourself and God. Those who do not teach love are false prophets.

Those who know love teach and serve love. God's will for us is that we use our free will to choose love in every moment.

In every instant we are determining that which we believe to be true about ourselves, the world around us, and our place in it.

That which we determine to be true for us (our belief), is molding and shaping our realities, both individually and collectively. However, there is only one truth, and that is love. All else is false, a lie, and what we are each being challenged to purge from our beings. To merge with the oneness of Divine Love is the ultimate mission for every soul.

We are given a conscience or higher self, so that we can discern truth (Love, God) from falsehood (a lie, the devil). Choosing of our own free will to adjust each thought, belief, feeling, action, and expression of being with love is atonement (at-<u>one</u>-ment) with God.

We align ourselves with God, Truth, Love, Law, and Justice through righteousness in thought, word, and deed.

Love is the only Right. Love is the only Truth. Love is the only Reality. Love is the only God. All else is false and fleeting and brings misery, pain, and despair, otherwise known as Hell. Both Heaven (True Reality) and Hell (False Reality) are found in perspective, which is shaped by belief.

Christ said, "If those who lead you say to you, 'See, the kingdom is in the sky,' then the birds of the sky will precede you. If they say to you, 'It is in the sea,' then the fish will precede you. Rather, the kingdom is inside of you, and it is outside of you. When you come to know yourselves, then you will become known, and you will realize that it is you who are the sons of the living father. But if you will not know yourselves, you dwell in poverty and it is you who are that poverty" (Gospel of Thomas).

When we receive things we don't like it's for our own good. This is so that we can learn right from wrong, truth from a lie, reality from fantasy, and make corrections to our beliefs and thus our course.

Like a good parent, Love is always acting in our best interest and providing us with exactly what we need, not want, for us to be the best person we can be.

The best you is the one that chooses to think, feel, and act from a place of Love. Not self-serving, but altruistic, self-sacrificing, unconditional love.

"There is no fear in love; but perfect love casteth out fear: because fear hath torment. He that feareth is not made perfect in love" (1 John 4:18).

Light casts shadows. Shadows are not the source of light and would not exist without it, therefore they are not real.

Shadows have no power apart from their creator; they cannot generate themselves. The light (good) creates the shadows (evil) but there are no shadows (evil) in it (good). Fear of what may be lurking in the shadows causes torment, great mental anguish, but pain eventually brings one to love.

Love is a tempering flame that burns away dross, by and by revealing the beauty within by purging ignorance.

Righteousness springs up from torment. We learn right from suffering wrong until our love is made perfect, and then fear is no longer in us.

"I am the Lord, and there is none else (there is nothing else and no one else), there is no God beside me (no other god or devil): I girded thee, though thou hast not known me: That they may know from the rising of the sun, and from the west, that there is none (no one else) beside me. I am the Lord, and there is none (not even one, no one) else. I form the light, and create darkness: I make peace, and create evil: I the Lord do all these things (no one else is doing them because no one else exists; God is the author, script, actors, and stage. Drop down, ye heavens, from above, and let the skies pour down righteousness: let the earth open, and let them bring forth salvation, and let righteousness spring up together; I the Lord have created it" (Isaiah 45: 5-8).

I believe God, the Creator of all, is the untainted energy of Perfect Love, the life-force that animates and drives all things, the No-Thing that creates Every-Thing, the ONE in the MANY, the Beginning and the End, the source of all, Divine Love. From this Perfect Love all things came forth, and to this Perfect Love all things will return, because True, Perfect, Divine Love is ALL there is, the Only Reality.

Belief in a lie, anything false, causes pain, and that pain is for our own good to bring us to righteousness (right seeing, right hearing, right thinking, right doing, which is love).

> Pain
> Falls like rain
> To help you grow.
> It comes into your life
> For a reason.
> Death in all forms,
> Visits everything born.
> All things have their season.

Love heals and purifies all things in the great cycles of time.

How to Find True Love and Lasting Happiness

The *Law of Attraction* states that *like action attracts like action*. This means you must genuinely be like that which you wish to attract. This is because you attract what you are, not what you desire; remember the law cannot be fooled.

To find true love you must become true love. You must make yourself like the person you wish to attract and stay together with.

If you want someone to love and accept you unconditionally, love and accept yourself unconditionally. If you want someone to always tell you the truth about how they feel, always tell the truth about how you feel. If you want someone who is faithful, be faithful. I could keep going but I think you get the point. Be for others what you wish others to be for you.

Every relationship is a mirror in which to see your own reflection. This is so that you can discover where you are in or out of balance with Love. As discussed in the previous chapter, Love is the only Truth, the only God, the only Reality.

Your feelings and criticisms about others are truths about yourself. They reflect how you yourself are being in that present moment.

Your judgments of others pinpoint where you need to make adjustments within yourself. They reveal exactly what you need to work on in order to purge falseness and embrace Love. This applies to how you feel in all relationships; with God, yourself, parents, siblings, children, friends, lovers, bosses, peers, co-workers, humanity, animals, nature, the planet, and even money.

Fear is the opposite of Love, not hate. Fear is ignorance, breads hate, and is the root of all that is evil or not good. Fear is not real; just as Franklin D. Roosevelt said, "The only thing we have to fear is fear itself."

Fear (evil) is the shadow of Love (good). Light casts shadows; the shadows are not real, only the Light is, but they look very real to those who live under them.

Just look at the word EVIL. What other words do the letters create? Veil, live, lie, vile. Evil is LIVE spelled backwards (just as DEVIL is LIVED spelled backwards). To believe in a lie is to live backwards, contrary to the truth.

Evil is a lie, a veil shrouding the truth that *Love is all there is.* Again, I will say, the only Truth is God and God is Love. Evil is the vileness within our own beings that chooses to feel, act, and live from a place of fear, our false master, instead of Love, our true Master.

Our challenge in every moment is to choose love over fear in all our ways.

Your self is the secret self you keep hidden, the one you desire for others to know deeply and love unconditionally. A soulmate relationship is one in which you feel like you can be 100% authentic, one in which you feel fully known and accepted.

If you attract a partner who is emotionally unavailable, it means that you are emotionally unavailable and need to learn how to open up and trust. If you attract someone who is jealous and possessive, it means you are jealous and possessive and need to learn how to stop trying to control how things turn out.

Whatever traits you judge to be in another are your traits. To change what you attract you must change yourself, period.

The key to finding your soulmate, self-love, and lasting happiness, is to make your own reflection true. This means not wearing any masks, not pretending to be who you think you need to be in order to make others happy, or to get them to love you. Make who you are on the inside match who you present yourself to be to the world, no dichotomy.

Until you love yourself enough to show your authentic self to everyone, can stop worrying about what others think, and don't need acceptance from them, you will never find your way home. Instead you will continue to attract events for your learning and partners who cannot be honest with you, because remember, *like action attracts like action.*

The whole function of the *Law of Attraction* or *Law of Love* is to show us to ourselves, and to eventually bring us to Divine Love through atonement (at-one-ment).

Every thought, word, action, and deed is accountable to Real Love, whether you know, like, or believe this or not. All you have to do is open your eyes in order to see it. If you can't you are blind; it's that obvious when you stop and look at yourself honestly.

Jesus said, "Recognize what is in front of your face, and what is concealed will be revealed to you. For there is nothing hidden that will not be disclosed" (Gospel of Thomas).

Identifying where we are out of balance with the will of Divine Love (which is for us to love), and making corrections to self-will, is what *Karma* is all about. "Love covers a multitude of sins" (1 Peter 4:8).

Love cancels out negative karma from the past, that then won't need to catch up to us later and teach us even harder lessons, because we resisted... that is if we have already voluntarily done the self-work, which is adjusting our will to the Divine Will, which is altruistic love.

The strongest attractions are to the people you are meant to learn your most valuable life lessons from, about who you really are and how you relate to yourself and the Creator (Divine Love).

These relationships are meant to make you question yourself, to ask the question why? They are almost always the ones that cause you the most angst. They come with an undeniable physical attraction, but also usually a lot of pain for the one most invested.

This is because it's not an equally reciprocated and committed love. Unbalanced relationships make you ask questions like "Why doesn't he or she love me back, or in the same way?" "Why does it hurt so bad to love this person?"

The person you are in an unequally reciprocated and unequally committed relationship is not your soulmate. This person is just meant to be in your life for a season, until your lesson with them about what True Love really is, and is not, has been learned.

Voluntarily choosing to learn, move on, and heal from these relationships, instead of hanging on and dragging them out for years, will bring one much closer to finding their life partner, self-love, and happiness, and will help it to happen even faster.

Be Clear to Find Self-Love

To find self-love you must learn to be CLEAR. The word clear becomes apparent in the search for self-love. Self-love requires confidence, like, esteem, acceptance and respect for who you are.

• Confidence requires trust, faith, reliance, assurance, and belief in your own abilities.

• Like requires that you are pleased with and enjoy being the person you are.

• Esteem requires that you consider your own opinion and course in life as valuable.

• Acceptance requires that you continually approve of and believe in who you are.

• Respect requires paying close attention to how you feel and regarding your own needs. You respect yourself when you can look back on your words, actions, and deeds and know that you have acted honorably, with integrity.

Clear shares a root with 'claim, declare, call out and counsel.' Today it translates as being 'transparent, easily seen or heard, not obscure, open, obvious, certain' and also 'free from guilt, free from debt, free from obstruction, free from impurities, innocent.'

To be clear you must not hide anything when declaring or making a claim. Implied by definition, you are innocent when speaking openly and honestly about whatever you feel inside, no matter what it is.

As long as you are being faithful to your current truth, that which your heart of hearts believes (and it is in alignment with selfless love and not selfishness) then you will not be punished for it.

The one great rule of love is DO NO HARM. And the way you do no harm, is to treat life as you would be treated.

The practice of being clear and speaking real words from the heart, as heard with the inner ear, will lead you to yourself, your soulmate, prosperity, and true and lasting happiness.

Real is translated as 'existing as or in fact, actual, true, genuine, authentic, honest, free from deceit.' To be real you must not lie, wear masks, or play roles.

Ear comes from 'perception, perceive', the root meaning being, 'to take hold of, feel, comprehend, to grasp mentally, recognize, observe, and be aware of.' To use your inner ear is to listen to your inner voice and pay attention to how your heart feels, specifically what your conscience or gut intuition is telling you.

Heart, besides being a vital muscle, is defined as being the 'innermost feelings or passion.' It is said to be the residing place of the soul, the guiding voice of the self, which can only be perceived through inner hearing.

The word heart is also connected etymologically, and is interchangeable, with the word courage. The Rumanian word for heart is inima and comes from the Latin anima, meaning soul. Inner hearing is awareness of how your heart/soul truly feels.

Everyone has heard the idioms, *heart-to heart-talk*, *follow your heart*, *listen to your heart*, and *speak from the heart*. To act from the heart is to use your inner ear to hear what your heart/soul is saying and then to do that thing.

The goal is to follow the conscience directive of selfless love, instead of that of the fear based animalistic ego, which is dominated by the instinct to preserve self at all costs.

To be CLEAR, you must have the courage to be REAL and to follow your conscience wherever it may lead. You hear your soul, the part of you that exists in the spirit realm, your higher-self or conscience, which receives its instructions from the Holy Spirit, through your inner ear, through paying attention to your feelings and motivations and checking them against selfless love.

Once you are clear with yourself about what is right for you, because it's based in real love and not selfishness, you must have the courage to act accordingly, which will bring you into harmony with Divine Love.

Herein lies your protection and prosperity. By making your own reflection clear, and by making selfless love the ruler of your moral code of conduct, you will find your soulmate, self-love, prosperity, stability, and lasting happiness.

Before speaking or acting, first stop and consider how you really feel. Hear the deepest messages of your conscience with your inner ear, and then have the courage to be honest about what you discover there. Always subject everything to the authority and service of unconditional, selfless Divine Love. If what you find in your heart is contrary to this love, then there is your self-work that needs to be done.

Stand by true love, which is Divine Love, in thought, word, and deed. Do what you feel is right for you based on what your conscience is telling you, regardless of what you fear the outcome might be. As long as you are hearing and serving Divine Love, you will be protected and provided for in all ways and will discover the *peace that passes understanding*.

All your actions must be rooted in altruistic love and must not cause harm. They must be as you would have done unto you, because what you put out you *will* get back.

It is not the true voice of your conscience if you are being urged to do harm to anything living, that which you would not want done to you. Those urges are based in fear and come from your ego and its need to preserve itself, the animal or beastly part of human nature that is directed by the survival of the fittest instinct: preservation of self at all costs.

Just like depicted in cartoons, there is forever a war being waged inside for control of your conscience in order to move you to act from a place of selfless-love (Christ-consciousness) or selfishness (Devil-consciousness), an angel or demon on each shoulder. Which will you allow to win?

Take Off Your Mask

True soulmates are partners who are clear mirrors to each other at all times. This is because they allow each other the space and freedom to be real. Soulmates do not place expectations on each other to fulfill one another's ideals of love. Soulmates also allow each other to grow and change.

Remain committed to you first, to being the person you really are, to being authentic, to making the person you present to the world the same as the person you are on the inside: no dichotomy. This will eventually draw your true love into your life through the *Law of Attraction*, another genuine person like the one you have become.

REALITY CHECK: Are you being clear with prospective mates, or are you playing roles and wearing masks that hide your true self? Are you afraid the real you will not be accepted? Are you looking for someone to fulfill your expectation of what you think love should be? If yes, it's time to take off your mask.

When you conceal how you really feel it's like wearing a mask. When two people are unable to be their true selves with one another, yet stay together, they create a prison of their own making which eventually must be escaped. Any relationship not founded on truth will crumble. Happiness can only come from love, and love does not lie.

When you are clear, you are like a still pond in which your reflection can be seen perfectly. When you are unclear, you are like a rippling pond in which only fragments of your reflection show.

You must have the courage to take off your mask. This requires speaking the truth you hear and feel coming from within your heart of hearts (your higher-self, your conscience) in any situation, no matter what you fear the outcome will be. Nothing real and lasting can stand on a lie.

If two people make a commitment to be authentic, they can turn their relationship into something that will stand the test of time, if also committed to treating each other as they desire to be treated. This also requires treating yourself as you would have others treat you.

Not being clear is choosing to say or do something other than what your heart is telling you; it is abandoning and not trusting who you are. Every time you choose to be unclear, to cover up your true feelings, you tear down your self-confidence, like, esteem, acceptance, and respect.

You are wearing a mask when you refuse to trust in or rely on your own abilities. This tears down your self-confidence.

You do not enjoy your own company, because who wants to be around liars or pretenders. This tears down your self-like.

You under value yourself by not considering your own opinion or course in life to be of importance. This tears down your self-esteem.

You repeatedly do not approve of or believe in your own character. This tears down your self-acceptance.

You do not honor or show consideration for your own feelings and needs. This tears down your self-respect.

Being unclear causes guilt, remorse, carries karmic debt, and creates obstructions and impurities in the self.

Tear etymologically comes from 'skin, hide.' To wear a mask is to *hide* your true feelings. It ultimately dates back to prehistoric Indo-European based sken- 'cut off, section, segment.'

Tearing yourself down is the same thing as cutting part of yourself off. Today it means to pull apart or separate into pieces, to divide with doubt, uncertainty, torment [a mind torn between duty (head) and desire (heart)].

At all times you have the choice to hear and honor your true-self by being clear, or to hide and tear yourself down by wearing a mask.

The root of tear, 'skin' hides the word 'sin.' Sin is linked etymologically to Latin sons 'guilty', to English sooth 'truth', and to Sanskrit satya- 'real, true.' The ancestral meaning of sin then is simply *to be guilty of not telling the truth.*

The other definition of tear is crying, weeping, sorrow, grief. The word grief comes from the root oppress, which is to subdue; repress emotions, feelings, passions. When you tear yourself down you create your own tears and grief by separating your head from your heart. You become divided.

Your head and heart must come together as soulmates; think of them as the male and female aspects of yourself, the male being the head and the female being the heart.

You must become your own soul's mate first, before you can be a soulmate to someone else. Only two whole people can come together in true love. To be whole you must know who you are and be committed to yourself first.

What causes you to wear a mask, to abandon your true self? The answer is fear. Fear is the cause for not speaking your truth, what you feel is right for you in any given situation based on the dictates of your conscience. Fear is always the reason for not choosing love.

Emotional pain is a result of fear and comes from not getting what you want, expect, or believe you need. Fear of pain, and the desire to avoid it, causes us to hide our hearts, to cut our true selves off, and to lie and hurt one another.

The only thing our free will affords us is the ability to choose. We cannot control everything that comes our way, but we do have the freedom to decide how we will react to it.

All choices boil down to two things, love (truth) or fear (a lie, sin), and elicit two things, action and reaction.

Fear is the antithesis of love and root of sin. Action motivated by fear always causes pain, every time, eventually, to the person committing the fearful act (and remember even thought is action).

This sets off a chain reaction of action/reaction events, because *every action creates an equal and opposite reaction*, Newton's *Third Law of Motion*. This vicious cycle will continue forever, or until so much pain has been caused to the doer that it is no longer wished to be experienced, and then a different choice will be made, one of selfless love instead of selfishness.

Choosing altruistic love creates a chain reaction of joy that breeds more joy. Joy is the result of choosing Love. It will endure as long as selfless love is the driving motivation behind all of your choices.

Recognize Your Programmed Ideal of Love and Release It

We all have an ideal of what we think love should be. This image is shaped by our family, friends, peers, culture, society, media, and the world at large.

When we grow up and enter into romantic relationships, we naturally look to our partner to fulfill our ideal of love.

Fear of possibly not achieving that ideal, of being let down by love (our own selfish version of love) if it doesn't happen to our satisfaction, tempts us into abandoning our true inner-selves, into putting on a mask and playing the role we think we must to be accepted and loved by others. Doing this is never loving yourself.

Fear etymologically meant 'danger, peril, ambush and snare,' with the basic sense of 'trap.' It is also linked to Greek 'pera', 'go through', and English fare, 'go', pointing to an underlying meaning of 'what one undergoes or experiences.' One of the meanings today is 'to expect with misgiving, doubt.'

The fear of not getting what you expect from love causes pain. Fear of pain and the desire to avoid it will tempt you into trying to snare someone into love with you.

You do this by telling them what you think they need to hear, or by presenting yourself as the person you believe they need you to be so that they will love you. I call this *Seductress Syndrome*, and it applies not only to romantic relationships, but to all relationships and what you desire to acquire from them.

Instead of falling into this trap, you must learn how to be who you really are at all times and to let those people who do not truly love you fall away. When you expect someone to fulfill your ideal of love it will only ever cause you pain.

Expectation comes from Latin 'expectare,' a compound of 'ex'- out and 'spectare' look. When you expect something, you are literally looking out for or anticipating it. When you place an expectation on someone, like your ideal of love, you are looking out to them (outside of yourself) for fulfillment.

Disappointment originally and literally meant, 'to deprive of an appointment; to fail to keep an appointment,' the ancestor of the modern English 'fail to satisfy an expectation, frustrate.'

I would like you to consider that when you are looking out to someone else to fulfill your ideal of love, you are actually dis-appointing yourself. You are missing your meeting with your true soulmate or destiny, which is ultimately the discovery of the Divine Love of God inside you.

Pain has an ancestral meaning of punishment and comes to English from Latin pen, 'penalty', which also gave us 'pine.' It originally meant pain. You create pain when you pine away for someone else to fulfill your expectation of love.

Pain is the result of looking outside of yourself for fulfillment. You must come to understand that when you expect someone else to fulfill your ideal of anything, it's really you who are causing your own disappointment from the very thing you desire.

Pain comes from expecting others to be who you need them to be instead of allowing them to be who they are. If you want someone to love you, allow them to be who they really are with no expectations. After all, isn't that what you want from a partner?

How can someone accept and love you for who you really are if you refuse to show them your true self? And if you can't accept and allow someone to be who they naturally are, how can you possibly expect them to fall in love with you? They will come to resent you instead.

Expecting your partner to be who you need them to be will eventually destruct any relationship. It is never fair and is not love to place your expectations on another; it is selfishness, plain and simple.

If you are doing this you are not giving the other person the Unconditional Love that you yourself seek. Again, the *Law of Attraction* or *Law of Love* states that *like action attracts like action*. You will always get what you give.

We expect from each other constantly, even without consciously realizing it. Once you recognize this behavior in yourself, you have a responsibility to stop doing it, and to assist others in doing the same.

Set the example and be a safe place where others can come to confide their true feelings without judgment, jealousy, blame, attack or attachment to how things will turn out.

You can only offer true love when you don't need someone else to be anything other than what they truly are. This is unconditional love, and the real meaning of *if you love something set it free.*

You do not truly love someone if you cannot allow them to be naturally who they are. The reverse is also true. If someone is not allowing you to be who you really are, then they are not truly loving you. Instead they are placing their false expectations of love on you, which is selfishness.

To know true love is to give it. You must learn to look at things as they really are, rather than as you would like them to be. You need to stop making yourself into what you think others need or want, and learn instead to find and stand by your authentic self.

Authenticity is required to find and fulfill your life's purpose, your heart's desire, that which will bring you true love and lasting happiness. This demands the constant practice of owning your feelings and expressing them without anger, judgment, blame, attack, or expectation.

Do not deny or repress your feelings, but instead communicate them accurately and openly, without feeling like you must apologize for them.

You must reach a point where you can face and experience what you desire, but can also let go of it if at any time holding on would cause you to dishonor the real you.

The practice of being authentic and treating life as you would have it treat you will eventually lead you to who you really are... to loving yourself, to your soulmate, to prosperity and stability, to your life's purpose, and to anything else you require to feel satisfied.

It may take much practice to get it right, and you may stumble and fall prey to temptations (not to be true to yourself) along the way, but do not lose your courage. It will eventually lead you to your destination, and you will be able to look back at all the pain and struggle and say "Oh, that's what it was for" and be thankful for it. You wouldn't trade it for anything.

The Truth Will Set You Free

It is a disservice to yourself and others when you are not completely honest and prolong a lie. THE TRUTH WILL SET YOU FREE and everyone else along with you.

You must learn to give that which you wish to receive. You cannot do this until you have worked through your own jealousy and fear, and are emotionally secure and able to communicate your feelings, desires, and concerns with honesty from a place of True Love.

The longer you hold on to someone that is not right for you because you fear the pain of loss, or think you might not find a better relationship, the longer your suffering will endure, and the longer your dis-appointment (not making your appointment with your heart's desire) will last.

Follow the path of truth which is practicing real love, and you will start to see that each new relationship will be better than the last. This is because you won't be repeating the same old mistakes.

Letting go will free you to move on. By releasing those people who cannot accept the real you, you will be opening the door for a more equal relationship to come into your life. The truer you are to yourself, the truer others will be to you.

Truth is Love and Love is Truth… There can be no love without truth, no truth without love. Think about it!

By consciously remembering the *Law of Attraction*, that *like action attracts like action*, and by doing unto others only what you want done back to you, you will eventually find happiness.

If your happiness requires a soulmate, one will be attracted, and you will know each other because you will each have followed your heart to the other by walking the *path of beauty* which is the path of selfless love and following the *Golden Rule*.

Four Rules to Live By

It all boils down to these four simple rules to live by. This is my interpretation of Angeles Arrien's *The Four Fold Way*. Following it will lead you to true love, self-love, and lasting happiness.

These four rules are all you need to know and practice in order to find your way in life. They are also known as the four rules of negotiation or peacemaking and can be applied to any relationship or situation to help bring about the highest good for everyone involved.

1. Be Present
2. Listen
3. Tell the Truth
4. Release Attachment to the Outcome

Explanation:

• Being present means showing up and being willing to be part of the solution. You have to be willing to hear the other party out and have a desire for resolution.

• Listening is truly hearing what someone is trying to tell you. You are not listening when you are thinking about your response, what you are going to say next to defend your own position and personal end goal.

• Telling the truth is communicating how you really feel at a heart (soul, higher-self, conscience) level, regardless of what you fear may be the result. The truth will always set you free to move to the next stage (even if telling it is scary), so just muster up the courage to do it!

• Releasing attachment to the outcome is having faith in God, letting go, and being willing to accept whatever happens as being for the best as long as you have acted from a place of Unconditional Love and followed the *Golden Rule*.

If you are attached to how things will turn out, you will not be able to do steps 1, 2, or 3. Attachment is selfishness, true love is acceptance. You must allow others to be who they truly are, and to give them the emotional and physical freedom to do what they feel is right for them (not you and your own selfish interests).

After all, isn't this what you really want from others, for them to be there for you, to care enough to show up, to hear you out, to always be honest about how they really feel, and to be willing to accept whatever you say is right for you, even if it's not what they want from or for you?

Again, to drive it home, *you must be willing to give to others what you wish to receive, and you must also be able to give it to yourself.*

Start practicing these four rules to live by and see how quickly things turn around for the better in your life. And never forget, the *Law of Attraction* or *Law of Love* (*like action attracts like action*) is always at work giving back to you that which you give to others.

Remember this in everything you do, and only ever give in thought, word, and deed that which you would have others give to you, and let it all serve unconditional, true, selfless, Divine Love.

Do this and your life will turn around. It will eventually become full of true love, prosperity, stability, and ever increasing happiness. You will wake up one day and realize that you have everything you need, that you always have had it, and you will be filled with a peace that passes understanding.

Always Remember

The finite cannot know the infinite in its totality, so it's prudent to be humble, lest you discover your knowledge to be folly and your worship idolatry.

To define the Creator is to limit God and bring Him-Her down to humanity's lowly estate. Creation can never contain, tell, or know the whole truth of the Creator. We catch only mere glimpses of shadows; we are but shadows of shadows under that Light. There is no end-all-be-all wisdom for humanity to ascertain beyond this: *Love is the cause, the key, the answer, the beginning and the end, all there is.*

In Love is the royal law fulfilled and all accomplished. God is Love. Love is God. Love is the will of God. Love is the law of God. Without Love all knowledge is rendered impotent.

If you will ask for forgiveness where you have trespassed against Divine Love, by serving and promoting your own self-image in the arrogance of your ignorance, you will be forgiven all your past karmic debt as long as you mean it and make a commitment to serve Divine Love selflessly going forward. All is vanity; all knowledge amounts to nothing without the key of love.

Humble yourself and love others, all of creation, as you would be loved, for this is how you love God, and your neighbor as yourself. It's the only Way, Truth, and Life that redeems, as Jesus so demonstrated once for all.

Belief in Jesus alone, without his selfless love guiding your thoughts, speech, and actions, is false belief. It's a broad way that leads to death of the soul (the second death) and many follow after it. Self-sacrificing love is the narrow path that leads to paradise.

Faith (belief) without works is dead. And works are thoughts, words, and deeds, all of which must be based in selfless love to be considered righteous. Acts performed to save the self are selfish and Anti-Christ (anti-love).

Belief in Jesus alone has not the power to save your soul, only Divine Love does, through your choice to serve it selflessly as Jesus did. You must follow after him, not just profess to serve him.

Jesus told his disciples, "If anyone would come after me, let him deny himself and take up his cross and follow me (Divine Love). For whoever would save his life will lose it, but whoever loses his life (gives up love of self-image) for my sake will find it. For what will it profit a man if he gains the whole world and forfeits his soul? Or what shall a man give in return for his soul?" (Matthew 16:24-26).

Christ is a title, a name given to the Divine Love of God. Christ is the unconditional, true, selfless love of God, His-Her only begotten son. Jesus was a son of man who demonstrated the perfect love of God in the flesh by being a pure vessel through which Divine Love (the Christ) could manifest, act and show forth a pattern unto humanity of the way it should go. Jesus, son of man, became a Son of God through his obedience to the true, unconditional, self-sacrificing, Divine Love of God. Only in

Divine Love is there found forgiveness, redemption, and resurrection.

In Levi Dowling's *The Aquarian Gospel of Jesus the Christ*, Jesus said, "What I have done all men can do, and what I am all men shall be."

Sin is everything that Love is not. In sin is death and in Love is eternal life.

"Beware of false prophets, which come to you in sheep's clothing, but inwardly they are ravening wolves (telling you that this belief or that belief, or belief in a name alone is enough). Ye shall know them by their fruits (their self-preserving acts). Do men gather grapes of thorns, or figs of thistles? Even so every good tree (selfless love) bringeth forth good fruit (works of selfless love); but a corrupt tree (selfishness) bringeth forth evil fruit (works for self). A good tree cannot bring forth evil fruit (it is impossible for selfless-love to perform selfish acts), neither can a corrupt tree bring forth good fruit (it is impossible for selfishness to be selfless). Every tree (soul) that bringeth not forth good fruit (selfless acts of love) is hewn down, and cast into the fire. Wherefore by their fruits (selfless or self-serving acts) ye shall know them. Not everyone that saith unto me, Lord, Lord (who says they believe in my name), shall enter into the kingdom of heaven; but he that doeth the *will* of my Father (Divine Love) which is in heaven. Many will say to me in that day, Lord, Lord, have we not prophesied in thy name? And in thy name have cast out devils? And in thy name done many wonderful works? And then will I profess unto them (those believers in my name), I never knew you (you who were motivated for self): depart from me, ye that work iniquity (all things selfish, anti-love). Therefore whosoever heareth these sayings of mine, and doeth them, I will liken him unto a wise man, which built his house (soul) upon a rock (Divine Love): And the rain descended, and the floods came, and the winds blew, and beat upon that house; and it fell not (from the estate of selfless love): for it was founded upon a rock (Divine Love). And every one that heareth these sayings of mine, and doeth them not, shall be likened unto a foolish man, which built his house upon the sand (selfishness): And the rain descended, and the floods came, and the winds blew, and beat upon that house (the one built on service to self); and it fell: and great was the fall of it (that soul)" (Matthew 7:15-27).

It is time to take a close hard look at ourselves, take an inventory of our morals and beliefs, to individually and collectively face and take responsibility for everything we are doing.

It is time to recognize our part in what we are creating and destroying. First in our own personal lives, and then in our families, communities, states, nations, and the planet. Before it's too late, before we can't pull back from the brink of extinction.

Love is the answer, and it starts with me and you. Here's how to take the first step. Ask yourself, "What am I doing or not doing that is causing harm to myself and others?" Others includes all things, Life itself. Ask the Creator to open your eyes. Make a list of the things that are anti-love and then change them.

We are all connected; nothing alive is self-sufficient. Nature demonstrates our interdependence on it and one another. Elect to stop doing things that inflict harm, because in hurting Life you are hurting yourself. And who really wants to do that? I hope you don't. I hope you will choose Love. I hope I will choose Love.

Those who do not see that we are ONE, bound together in the fate of Nature's survival, that we are part of Life itself, and that creation is evolving... Those who cannot see that we are all connected, that man is a species existing in a vast ocean of species, and that we all need each other... Those who believe we stand apart from Nature (the rest of creation) and are not dependent on or bound by its laws... and thus take from Life what they will and do with it as they please with no regard... are blind to their own selfish ignorance and the harm they are causing to themselves and others.

Those who do not fear the ramifications of their own actions, who do not know we are held accountable by Natural and Universal Laws which God put in place, are beasts running on animal instinct, a survival of the fittest mentality. They are lost in the darkness of ignorance, believing they are already found in their temporary worldly success. They believe they are chosen, special, called, entitled to rule, free to live for themselves, robbing, raping and pillaging our inheritance.

"Father, forgive them; for they know not what they do" (Luke 23:34). "For all the law is fulfilled in one word, even in this; Thou shalt *love* thy neighbor as thyself" (Galatians 5:14).

The Quest

Your black tower calls in my brightest hour,
Pleading for me to keep my own power,

Whispering come back, by false love be
subdued,
But I know in that place I will not be renewed.

So I raise my shield and stand in what's real,
Protecting myself from all that you feel,

Raw emotions that churn your mind like a
wheel,
As it plots how to keep my heart it would steal.

I too there wept at the glory of He,
And sang with the angels to set Him free,

As hung He there dying on that cross,
For the sins of the world as we cried for our
loss.

I kept slaves in bondage as Queen of the Nile,
Was there at the start to see Adam smile.

Tasted the fruit that the serpent did offer,
And carried the blame for why all men suffer.

Yes my love, the Quest is eternal,
And to it we're bound, the urge calls supernal.

The moment is now, there is no other,
So put down your hate and become a lover.

Indeed God is ALL, oh yes God is One,
Yet in so many sights He still seems undone.

How can I rest, go off to star in some play,
When so many others cry on this day?

How can I lay my sword on the ground,
Walk away from the light in my heart that's
been found,

From the cause that rings true and in my soul
cries,
The one that brings tears of joy to my eyes?

The time is now, the time for might,
To stand up and shout, this is what's right.

To love one another, not each make our own
mark,
For that path is separate, alone in the dark.

It is in truth, this song I must follow,
My dear sweet one, for all else is hollow.

My Prayer

Thank you, unfathomable womb in which we create, for the knowledge you so freely give when asked, about from where and why things come.

Praise be to you for sight, as I stand in the veil of seeming reality, eyes wide open, letting in the truth.

I find peace in the wisdom of knowing what to want. As the hands of destiny and free-will clasp, I offer myself in service to the highest good.

You are my comforter when the Harvester approaches to reap His bounty, as I prepare to navigate the road of seeming opposites.

Thank you for the light of love, may it shine as a beacon to others who now walk on roads dim-lit, screaming out "WHY?" in pain.

I hold my urn unto the sky and ask that it be filled for pouring, on to others passing by, as the wheel of life keeps turning.

My will is Thy Will; what is Thy Will for me today? And right away you say, "Just BE Love."